THE AUTHOR'S GUIDE TO VELLUM

Creating Beautiful Books with Vellum 2.0

CHUCK HEINTZELMAN

Contents

Conventions Used in This Book   v

1. Introduction   1
2. Getting Vellum   5
3. The Big Picture   8
4. Importing Your Manuscript   13
5. The Title Info   22
6. The Ebook Cover   27
7. Vellum Elements   32
8. The Title Page   51
9. Book Styles   56
10. Preview   66
11. Page Numbers   72
12. Table of Contents   75
13. Text Features   81
14. Using Images   90
15. Exporting to RTF   98
16. Generating Ebooks   104
17. Creating Print Books   109
18. Creating Ebook Box Sets   118
19. What Vellum Cannot Do   128
20. Tips and Tricks   130
21. Using MacinCloud   136

Also by Chuck Heintzelman   141
About the Author   143
About BundleRabbit   145
Example Bundles at BundleRabbit   147

Conventions Used in This Book

Several typographical conventions are used throughout this book.

Small caps are used for items on your computer

Whether it's a menu item, a button you click, or an option presented to you, SMALL CAPS are used indicate a value you'll see on your computer's screen. Additionally, **BUTTONS** are bold-faced.

Italicized small caps are used for screens or areas in your software

Both small caps and italicized text refer to settings or dialog boxes in Vellum. *TABLE OF CONTENTS SETTINGS* or the *NAVIGATOR* are examples of this.

Elements are capitalized and italicized

Elements are the building blocks of Vellum. Each *Element* is listed in the *NAVIGATOR*. (The *NAVIGATOR* is explained in **Chapter 3 – The Big Picture.**) Any time an *Element* is mentioned when referring to these building blocks, or a specific *Element* such as a *Dedication* is mentioned, the word is capitalized and italicized.

Paragraphs ending with ...

When you're reading along and notice a paragraph ends with ellipses (...), this indicates an image is immediately following the paragraph. If you're reading the ebook version of *The Author's Guide to Vellum*, whether the image immediately follows the paragraph or is moved to the next page depends on the device you're reading on.

ONE

Introduction

This chapter provides a brief introduction to Vellum, what it does, and who created it.

What is Vellum?

V ellum is a software package that helps you create books. It allows you to package your manuscript as an ebook or print book.

Sounds pretty simple, doesn't it?

It is simple. And the software is elegantly designed. It's a joy to use.

But I heard Vellum only works on Mac computers?

Well, technically, yes, Vellum only runs on Apple macOS 10.11 or newer. But if you're a Windows or Linux user, you can use the MacinCloud service and run Vellum for $1 per hour. See the **Chapter 21 – Using MacinCloud** for details.

What Vellum Does

The purest, most honorable goal of software is to make your life better. If you're an indie author, Vellum does exactly this.

Vellum imports your manuscript and, with a few clicks, generates ready-to-upload ebooks for every major ebook retailer. And now with Vellum 2.0, you can also generate print books.

Vellum makes your life better by

- making it easy and simple to create ebooks
- creating the interior file for paperbacks
- saving you hours of formatting time
- generating a final product that is simply stunning

Vellum's purpose is summed up best by its motto:

CREATE BEAUTIFUL BOOKS

We're long past the initial days of the indie revolution when an author could create a quick ebook, maybe push their Word manuscript through Smashword's *Meat Grinder* to get the MOBI file, slap on any ol' cover, and then upload the ebook to Amazon. Well, I suppose you could still do that, but your sales will be affected.

Today's readers are more discerning. They expect a professional-looking ebook.

Today's readers expect the quality that Vellum produces.

Who's Behind Vellum

The creators of Vellum are Brad West and Brad Andalman—known collectively as "The Two Brads." They both formerly worked for Pixar, each with more than a decade of experience developing software and building animation systems used on films like *Finding Nemo*, *The Incredibles*, and *Toy Story 2*.

How cool is it that they built software at Pixar to help creators build beautiful animations? Now they're doing the same in a different industry. Now they help authors create beautiful books.

In 2012, The Two Brads created a company named **180g** (which I always think of as 180 grams, but that's probably not what it means). 180g is the company behind Vellum.

My Credentials

Who am I and why can I teach you about Vellum?

My name is Chuck Heintzelman. I'm a software developer, a writer, and—for the last couple years—an ebook bundler. I created and run the service at BundleRabbit.com. BundleRabbit allows anyone to become a "curator" and build multi-author ebook bundles. BundleRabbit has an ebook marketplace where hundreds of authors have uploaded their ebooks. Curators can choose ebooks from this marketplace, organize the ebooks into a bundle, enter sales copy for the bundle, upload a cover, and then... PUBLISH THE BUNDLE.

BundleRabbit distributes 70% of each sale across all the authors in the bundle. Plus a little *sumpin' sumpin'* for the curator.

Behind the scenes at BundleRabbit several things happen when a bundle is published. One of them is building the bundle. To do this, I use Vellum, because it literally takes only 5 to 10 minutes to drag and drop individual ebooks into Vellum and create a box set suitable for publishing at Kobo, Amazon, Barnes & Noble, and iBooks.

And the box sets produced by Vellum are simply amazing. The quality is unsurpassed.

I've created more than 80 bundles (box sets) at BundleRabbit in the last year.

Unfortunately, Vellum doesn't allow normal ebooks (EPUBs and MOBIs) to be imported to create a box set. Nope. You have to use ebooks built with Vellum. (You can drag and drop multiple DOCX files into Vellum, but then you must edit the imported text.)

Which means at BundleRabbit I must covert each ebook to be bundled to Vellum. As of this morning I have converted almost 700 ebooks.

When you add together the number of ebooks I've converted to Vellum for BundleRabbit, the number of box sets I've created, and the number of ebooks I've created in Vellum for my personal work.

I Have Created More Than 900 Ebooks In Vellum

You could say I know a little about this software.

TWO

Getting Vellum

This chapter explains how to download and install Vellum. Various purchase options are also discussed.

Downloading Vellum

To get a copy of Vellum and install it on your computer go to vellum.pub and click the **DOWNLOAD** button…

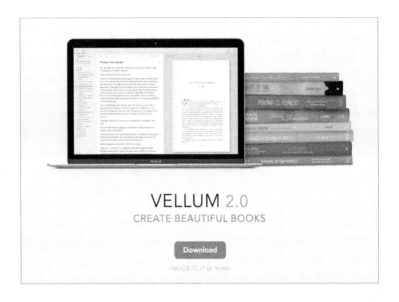

This will download a file named VELLUM-INSTALLER.ZIP to your computer. Use Finder to locate this file in your DOWNLOADS directory and double-click on it to extract the contents. Now you'll have a file named VELLUM INSTALLER.APP.

Double-click VELLUM INSTALLER.APP and follow the prompts to install Vellum on your computer.

Limitations of the Download

The file you download is fully functional except for one thing. You cannot "Generate" the books. This means you can import Word DOCX files, add and edit pages within the book, save the book, and even preview the book.

You just cannot create the EPUB, MOBI, or print file. To do that, you have to purchase Vellum (see below).

If you haven't purchased Vellum, I urge you to download it

and play around with it. You'll be able to test out almost every aspect of the program.

Purchase Options

Vellum used to have what they called "Ebook Credits." This allowed you to purchase the generation of 1, 5, or 10 ebooks. Yep, one of the ways 180g monetized Vellum was to charge for each and every ebook you created. But you did have the option to buy the "unlimited" package to generate as many ebooks as you desired. 180g eliminated this program. Don't worry, though. If you purchased "Ebook Credits" in the past, they will still work until you run out of credits.

Today, you have two options to purchase Vellum:

1. Purchase **Vellum Ebooks** for $199.99. This version of the Vellum software allows you to generate an unlimited number of ebooks.
2. Purchase **Vellum Press** for $249.99. This version allows you to generate unlimited ebooks and unlimited paperbacks.

This might seem like a lot of money for software, but after you understand the power of Vellum, you'll see it'd still be a bargain at twice the price.

And in a world where it seems like every piece of software is moving to a subscription model where you must pay a monthly or yearly fee (ahem, Photoshop), isn't it nice to have software you pay for only once?

THREE

The Big Picture

This chapter describes the major areas of Vellum's user interface, explains how Vellum organizes ebooks, and presents the five steps of the publishing workflow when using Vellum.

The Areas of Vellum's User Interface

When you are working with an ebook in Vellum, the screen has four major areas...

1 – The Top Bar

There's probably a more official name for this area, but I always call it the *Top Bar*. Here's where you can toggle the display of the *Navigator* (area #2) and the *Preview* (area #4). This is also where the **Generate** button lives.

2 – Navigator

This area along the left edge of the software is called the *Navigator*. It shows you where you are within the book you're working on. The *Navigator* allows you to quickly navigate through your entire book.

3 – Text Editor

This area allows you to make changes to the text, insert Text Features such as *Ornamental Breaks* or *Store Links*, apply font effects such as bold and italics, and perform other editing tasks such as doing a spelling check.

4 – Preview

This area shows you what your book will look like across a variety of devices. You can also see what the print version looks like in the *Preview*.

How Vellum Structures Books

Vellum organizes your book into *Elements*, and you can see each element in the *Navigator*. The most common element is a *Chapter*, but there are a number of specialty elements such as *About the Author* or *Copyright*.

There are two special *Elements* that can contain other *Elements*: *Volumes* and *Parts*.

A *Part* can contain any other type of *Element* except for *Volumes*. They are useful when your manuscript is divided into large sections such as PART ONE, PART TWO, etc.

A *Volume* can contain any other type of *Element* except other

Volumes. The *Volume Element* is useful for creating box sets.

In the snippet of the *NAVIGATOR* displayed below, there are three *Volumes*: *Silent Victor, Alien Influences*, and *Star Rain*. The *Star Rain Volume* is expanded and you can see the following elements: *Title Page, Dedication, Part I, Part II*, and *Part III*. And within the expanded *Part I* there are five *Elements: Prologue, One, Two, Three*, and *Four*.

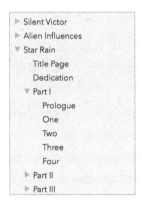

The Vellum Publishing Workflow

When using Vellum, there are five steps in the publishing workflow…

Step 01 – Build

The first step is to build the book. You can import your manuscript, update the book's title and other information, upload a cover, and add special *Elements* such as *Copyright* or *About the Author.* You can check the spelling and perform other rudimentary editing tasks.

Step 02 – Style

After the content is built, you choose from one of eight different *BOOK STYLES*. The style specifies how the book will appear when generated.

Step 03 – Preview

Using Vellum's *PREVIEW,* you can check to see what your book will look like on a Kindle. Or on an iPhone. Or any of seven different devices. You can also preview what the print version of your book will look like.

———

The *PREVIEW* is one of the greatest Vellum features!

Never again will you wonder what your ebook looks like on a iPhone, because with Vellum you can easily preview the appearance.

———

Step 04 – Generate

Once your book looks good, you click the **GENERATE** button. This allows you to create the files for Kobo, Kindle, iBooks, Nook, Google Play, and a Generic EPUB version for other sites such as Smashwords, Draft2Digital, and BundleRabbit. You can also generate the Interior PDF for use at CreateSpace, Nook Press, or IngramSpark.

Step 05 – Upload

The last step in the workflow is to upload the files to each platform you're publishing on. In other words, you take the MOBI file generated for Kindles and upload it to your KDP account. You upload the Kobo EPUB to Kobo Writing Life. And so on.

This step happens outside Vellum, but is included in the publishing workflow to illustrate the complete picture.

FOUR

Importing Your Manuscript

This chapter explains the process of importing your manuscript into Vellum.

You Start With a DOCX

V ellum requires your manuscript be in DOCX format in order to import it. If you're using Microsoft Word, then most likely it is already in this format. If not, you can save your manuscript as a DOCX by selecting the FILE menu and then SAVE AS...

This will present you with the *Save* dialog box. Make sure to change the File Format to "Word Document (.docx)" before clicking the **Save** button...

How Vellum Detects Chapters

Vellum is pretty good at figuring out where to break your manuscript into *Chapters*, but you may find it needs a little help on occasion. If so, you can give Vellum hints to help it detect the *Chapters* in your manuscript. Vellum's online help (http://help.vellum.pub) lists the clues Vellum uses to detect chapters in your manuscript:

- A page break before the title of a chapter
- More than three empty paragraphs in a row
- Centered, bold text
- Centered, bold text that begins with the word **Chapter**
- Titles of standard elements such as **Epilogue** or **Acknowledgements**

Compiling Scrivener to DOCX

If you use Scrivener to write your manuscript, you can compile the manuscript to a DOCX by selecting the File menu and choosing Compile...

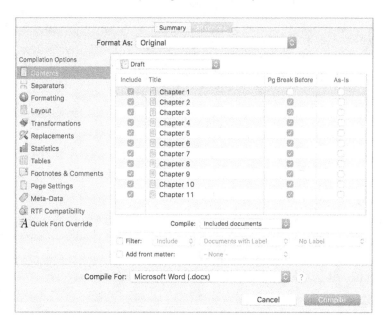

Make sure the ALL OPTIONS tab is selected in the *COMPILE* dialog box. Then set COMPILE FOR to "Microsoft Word (.docx)" before clicking the **COMPILE** button.

Also notice in the example there's a PG BREAK BEFORE each chapter to help Vellum detect the chapters.

Exporting to DOCX from Pages

If your manuscript is written with Pages, you can easily export it to DOCX by selecting the FILE menu and choosing EXPORT TO > WORD... Then from the *EXPORT YOUR DOCUMENT* dialog box, under ADVANCED OPTIONS, make sure the FORMAT is ".docx" before clicking the **NEXT...** button...

Vellum's Custom Styles

If you write your manuscript in Microsoft Word, another option is to use Vellum's Custom Styles. I often use this approach because there is far less tweaking in Vellum after importing the DOCX.

Download Vellum's Documents

To get started, download the documents Vellum provides from the following URL:

https://get.180g.co/download/VellumAdvancedImportDocuments.zip

Use Finder to locate this file in your Downloads folder. Double-click to extract the contents and then you'll see two files in the VELLUM ADVANCED IMPORT DOCUMENTS folder:

- VELLUM ADVANCED IMPORT GUIDE.DOCX – You can open this file with Word for examples of each style.
- VELLUM BOOK STYLE.DOTX – This is a Word template file containing the special Vellum styles

Creating a Word Vellum Template File

To make it easy to create new Word documents using Vellum's Custom Styles, I suggest creating a Vellum template that's available when you create new Word documents.

First double-click on the VELLUM BOOK STYLE.DOTX file, which you downloaded and extracted earlier. This will open the file in Microsoft Word. Then choose the FILE menu and choose SAVE AS TEMPLATE...

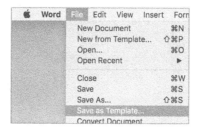

Then from the *SAVE* dialog box, change SAVE AS to Vellum.dotx...

Once you do this, the next time you start Word (or choose FILE > NEW FROM TEMPLATE...) you'll see a new template called **Vellum** from which you can create a new Word document...

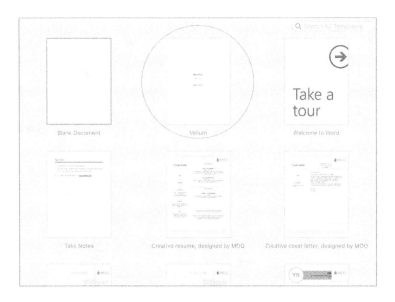

When you use this new template, you'll have an additional 17 Vellum styles available. Each of the styles begin with "Vellum."

The 17 Vellum Styles

Here's a brief overview of each style available and how to use it.

1. *Vellum Attribution* – This style is used to mark the attribution for block quotes or verses.
2. *Vellum Author* – Use this style on the author's name if you have a title page in your manuscript.
3. *Vellum Block Quote* – Mark quotations in your manuscript with this style. Use the *Vellum Attribution* to mark who the quote is from.
4. *Vellum Book Subtitle* – Use this for your book's subtitle, if you have a title page.

5. *Vellum Book Title* – If you have a title page, use this style for the book's title.

6. *Vellum Chapter Subtitle* – If you subtitle your chapters, use this style on the subtitle.

7. *Vellum Chapter Title* – Mark each chapter within your manuscript with this style.

8. *Vellum Chapter Title (with Subtitle)* – If your chapters have subtitles, use this style on each chapter title instead of the *Vellum Chapter Title.*

9. *Vellum Dedication Text* – Mark the text on your dedication page with this style.

10. *Vellum Epigraph Text* – If you have an epigraph page in your manuscript, use this style for the text.

11. *Vellum Flush Left* – Use this style on paragraphs to align them left, with no indent.

12. *Vellum Ornamental Break* – Use this style on the divider at scene breaks. If you use three asterisks (* * *) for scene breaks, Vellum almost always detects them as a break, but if you use some other text for scene breaks be sure and mark them with this style.

13. *Vellum Part Subtitle* – If your manuscript is divided into *Parts*, use this style on any subtitle for the *Part.*

14. *Vellum Part Title* – Use this style to mark the title of each *Part* in your manuscript.

15. *Vellum Part Title (with Subtitle)* – Use this style instead of the *Vellum Part Title* if your manuscript's *Parts* contain subtitles.

16. *Vellum Subheading* – This style can be used on subheadings within your text.

17. *Vellum Verse* – This style is useful for poetry. Mark the entire poem with this style and add the attribution with the *Vellum Attribution* style.

———

THERE ARE TWO TYPES OF BREAKS

Vellum uses two types of breaks: *Ornamental Breaks* and blank space breaks. Mark where you want *Ornamental Breaks* with the *Vellum Ornamental Break* style (or use the standard centered * * * text on a line by itself). If you have one or more blank paragraphs in your text, Vellum will interpret that as a blank space break.

Importing the DOCX

When you first start Vellum, you'll see a screen that shows the recent Vellum files you've worked with along the right side...

Click on the **IMPORT WORD FILE...** button and navigate to the DOCX you're importing, and click the **IMPORT** button.

That's it. Your manuscript has been imported.

Pretty easy.

Another method to import DOCX files is to create a blank Vellum project and then drag and drop DOCX files directly into the *Navigator*.

The first thing you should do after importing a DOCX is to press Cmd+S and save your new Vellum project.

Then next thing you need to do is go through your Vellum project, fix any *Chapters* Vellum didn't cleanly import, and add any missing *Elements*.

FIVE

The Title Info

_____

T his chapter explains how to access and update title, author, and other global information about your book.

What is the Title Info?

The *TITLE INFO* is the title, subtitle, author name(s), and other information Vellum keeps track of for your book. The *TITLE INFO* becomes part of your ebook's metadata (information inside your ebook describing the book).

When you generate a print version of your book, the title and author from the *TITLE INFO* is used on the page headers.

How to Access the Title Info

To access the *TITLE INFO* simply click the title of your book at the top of the *NAVIGATOR*...

Once you click on title in the *NAVIGATOR*, the *TEXT EDITOR* will change. At the top there are two tabs. Make sure the TITLE INFO tab is selected…

This will show you the *TITLE INFO*…

Your Book's Title Page

The information you enter for TITLE, SUBTITLE, AUTHOR, CONTRIBUTORS, PUBLISHER, PUBLISHER LINK, and PUBLISHER LOGO are used to automatically create your book's *Title Page…*

THE INVISIBLE MAN
A GROTESQUE ROMANCE

H. G. WELLS

If you don't specify a PUBLISHER LOGO in the *TITLE INFO*, the PUBLISHER NAME appears on the *Title Page* instead of the logo. For ebooks, the PUBLISHER LOGO (or PUBLISHER NAME) will be a web link to the PUBLISHER LINK.

About the Metadata

The ebooks Vellum generates contain metadata information based on the information you enter for the TITLE INFO.

- The TITLE and the SUBTITLE (if any) are combined to form the ebook's internal *Title*.
- The AUTHOR is added as the *Creator* with an *Author* role.
- Each CONTRIBUTOR is also added as a *Creator*, and their roles (Author, Editor, Illustrator, etc.) are associated with their names.
- The LANGUAGE is stored in the ebook's *Language* metadata.
- The ebook's *Rights* are built from the current year and the AUTHOR. For me, the *Rights* metadata would read "Copyright 2017 Chuck Heintzelman. All rights reserved."
- The PUBLISHER NAME is stored in the metadata for *Publisher*.

Although most readers are unaware this metadata exists in their ebooks, programs such as Calibre and iBooks use this data to help keep the reader's electronic library organized.

Some stores will also use this metadata for search and organizational purposes.

Specifying Multiple Creators

With Vellum it is easy to add multiple creators to your book. Simply click the (**+**) after CONTRIBUTOR and fill in the details.

If you click on AUTHOR in the Contributors section, you can pick a different role for the person than the standard Author role.

Each contributor you add will appear on the *Title Page* Vellum generates for your book. And, as stated earlier, each CONTRIBUTOR is added to the ebook's metadata.

SIX

The Ebook Cover

This chapter explains how to add a cover image to your ebook in Vellum.

How to Access the Ebook Cover

You access the EBOOK COVER the same way as you accessed the TITLE INFO, by clicking your book's title at the top of the NAVIGATOR. But instead of clicking the TITLE INFO tab, you need to select the EBOOK COVER tab...

When the EBOOK COVER tab is selected, you'll see the ebook's cover (if there is one) and a feedback message underneath it...

Adding or Replacing the cover

If you hover your mouse over the cover, it will show a large (**+**) on the cover image…

This (**+**) indicates you can click to add a cover. When you click it, Vellum will allow you to navigate through your files and pick the cover image to use.

Another method is to simply drag and drop your cover file onto Vellum's image of the ebook's cover.

Once you select a valid cover, the feedback message will indicate the cover is valid...

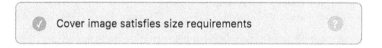

About the Cover Image

You can upload almost any type of image for the cover. TIFF, PNG, JPEG, and GIF are all valid formats. But Vellum recommends using a lossless format (meaning the quality does not decrease during compression). The lossless formats are TIFF and PNG.

Vellum embeds the cover image in the ebooks it creates. If a reader flips to the beginning of the book, they'll see the cover.

When you generate ebooks, Vellum will output a cover image for each ebook platform. In other words, if you generate ebooks for Kobo and Amazon, there will be a Kobo.jpg and an Amazon.jpg, which you can then upload to Kobo Writing Life and Kindle Direct Publishing.

Vellum ensures each vendor specific cover image meets the requirement for the vendor.

Size Requirements

The basic rule for cover images is that the height must be at least 2500 pixels. The minimum width varies depending on the aspect ratio of your book.

Vellum recommends the following dimensions for the most common aspect ratios:

- *1:1.33 Ratio* – 1880 x 2500 pixels
- *1:1.5 Ratio* – 1667 x 2500 pixels
- *1:1.6 Ratio* – 1563 x 2500 pixels

It doesn't hurt to upload images that are larger than these minimums. Since Vellum creates vendor specific cover images, it will produce the best size image for each vendor.

If you upload a cover image that is too small, the feedback message will notify you.

Cover image is too small
1667 x 2500 or larger is recommended

SEVEN

Vellum Elements

This chapter explains the Vellum Elements and what makes each Element unique.

What Are Elements?

V ellum *Elements* are the building blocks of your book. Each distinct *Element* appears in the *NAVIGATOR* and may appear in the *Table of Contents*. The most common *Element* is a *Chapter*.

Some *Elements* have unique features, such as *About the Author*, which allows you to enter your social media links.

Below is a handy chart that lists each *Element* type and the treatment the *Element* receives…

Element	In TOC	Start Page	Heading	Top Margin	Notes
Chapter	Yes	Yes	Styled	Large	Paragraph Styles
Blurbs	No	No	Plain	Small	No Paragraph Styles
Copyright	No	No	None	Small	No indents, Vellum flag
Dedication	No	No	None	Always Large	Centered, italic text
Epigraph	No	No	None	Always Large	No Paragraph Styles
Foreword	Yes	Yes	Plain	Large	No Paragraph Styles
Introduction	Yes	Yes	Plain	Large	No Paragraph Styles
Preface	Yes	Yes	Plain	Large	No Paragraph Styles
Prologue	Yes	Yes	Styled	Large	Paragraph Styles
Epilogue	Yes	Yes	Styled	Large	Paragraph Styles
Afterword	Yes	Yes	Plain	Large	No Paragraph Styles
Acknowledgments	Yes	Yes	Plain	Large	No Paragraph Styles
About the Author	Yes	Yes	Plain	Small	No Paragraph Styles, Author info
Also By	Yes	Yes	Plain	Small	Centered text
Uncategorized	Yes	Yes	Plain	Large	No Paragraph Styles
Part	Yes	Yes	Styled	Large	No Paragraph Styles
Volume	Yes	Yes	Styled	Large	No Paragraph Styles

Here's a quick description of each column in the above table.

- **Element** – The name of the Vellum *Element*.
- **In TOC** – Does the *Element* appear in the book's *Table of Contents*?
- **Start Page** – Can the *Element* be the Start Page? The first *Element* in your book that can be a Start Page will be the position in the ebook a reader will automatically go to when they open the ebook.
- **Heading** – How the *Element's* heading is treated. "None" means the heading is not displayed by default. "Plain" specifies the heading receives no special styling. It is centered near the top of the page. "Styled" indicates the heading may have special flourishes as defined by your *BOOK STYLE*.
- **Top Margin** – Describes the margin before the heading and before the text begins on the page. When you hide the heading, normally the *Element's* text begins at the very top of the page. But the *Dedication* and *Epigraph Elements* are special. They always have a

large margin above the text, whether the heading is displayed or not.

- **Notes** – Special notes about the *Element*. These are described in more detail below, in the sections for each *Element*.

———

If an *Element* has Paragraph Styles, then it receives the FIRST PARAGRAPH and PARAGRAPH AFTER BREAK styles from the BOOK STYLE. (See **Chapter 9 – Book Styles.**) If the *Element* does not have Paragraph Styles, then the first paragraph and the paragraph after a break have no indent —unless the *Element* has a special treatment for the text.

———

The Chapter Element

Vellum keeps track of *Chapter* numbers for you. When you import a DOCX, Vellum notices headings like "Chapter 1" or "Chapter One" and removes them, relying instead on its own *Chapter* numbering. If you don't specify a heading for your chapters, or Vellum removes them during the import, they will display as *Chapter 1, Chapter 2,* and so forth.

But you can type in the heading yourself at the top of the TEXT EDITOR...

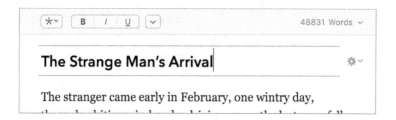

When you specify your own *Chapter* headings, Vellum still tracks the number and displays the *Chapter* in the NAVIGATOR and on the *Table of Contents* with the number before the title…

You can change this behavior by going into the ELEMENT SETTINGS, which is accessed by clicking on the gear icon at the top right of the TEXT EDITOR…

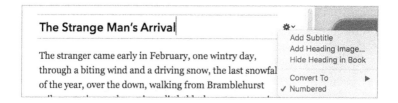

Just uncheck the NUMBERED option from this menu.

ELEMENT SETTINGS is also where you can add a subtitle to the chapter.

Chapter Elements receive the HEADING style from the *BOOK STYLE*. The paragraphs are also styled, which means *Chapters* receive the FIRST PARAGRAPH and PARAGRAPH AFTER BREAK treatment from the *BOOK STYLE*.

Depending on your use of titles, subtitles, and numbering, *Chapters* can appear in your book a variety of ways.

Below are three different examples…

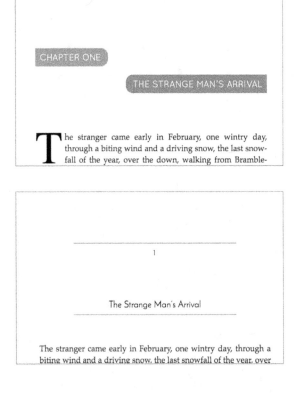

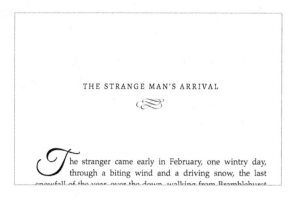

The Blurbs Element

The primary use for *Blurbs* is to add quotes about the author and/or book. Usually, it's a long page of Block Quotes.

Blurbs do not appear in the *Table of Contents*, there is a small top margin, and there's no special paragraph styling.

Below are examples of *Blurbs*…

PRAISE FOR CHUCK HEINTZELMAN

Charles Heintzelman writes from the heart and hits you in the gut.

— YOUR #1 FAN

Stunning!

— THAT GUY WHO'S ALWAYS AT STARBUCKS

Charles Heintzelman has given the world a stellar debut.

— FELLOW AUTHOR

TIP: Repurpose Elements As Needed

You can use any *Element* for any purpose. There are no absolute rules for any *Element*. For example, let's say you want a "Where To Find Me Online" page near the front of your book and you don't want this to appear in your *Table Of Contents* and you want it before the *Table Of Contents* appears in your book. Easy. Simple add a *Blurbs Element* to your ebook, retitle it as "Where To Find Me Online" and enter the content in the *Text Editor*.

The Copyright Element

This *Element* is used to display publication, legal, and copyright information. *Copyrights* do not appear in the Table of Contents, the top margin is small, and the title and paragraphs of the page have no special styling.

The text on *Copyright Elements* are handled differently than the other *Elements*. No paragraphs are indented and their justification is ragged right. Often people will apply an Alignment Block to the text in a *Copyright* to have it centered on the page. See **Chapter 13 - Text Features** for information about Alignment Blocks.

There is a special feature of the *Copyright* element, a checkbox at the bottom of the TEXT EDITOR titled INCLUDE CREATED WITH VELLUM...

Copyright   ⚙ ˅

Copyright © 2017 by Charles Heintzelman

All rights reserved.

No part of this book may be reproduced in any form or by any electronic or mechanical means, including information storage and retrieval systems, without written permission from the author, except for the use of brief quotations in a book review.

☑ Include **Created with Vellum**

If INCLUDE CREATED WITH VELLUM is checked a little "Created

with Vellum" notice will appear at the bottom of your copyright page with a link to http://vellum.pub.

Note that the INCLUDE CREATED WITH VELLUM is automatically checked when you add the *Copyright Element*, so if you don't want it you must be sure to uncheck it. This is especially important if you're repurposing a *Copyright Element* for some other use other than displaying the copyright.

For print books, *Copyrights* are aligned with the bottom of the printed page.

The Dedication Element

Books often have a dedication page somewhere near the front of the book. Use the *Dedication Element* for this purpose.

By default, the title does not display for *Dedications* and the top margin is always large whether the title is displayed or not. *Dedications* do not appear in the *Table of Contents*.

The text is treated special on *Dedications*. Paragraphs are centered and italicized.

Notice the large top margin in the example *Dedication* below…

For my Family

The Epigraph Element

The *Epigraph* is often a quotation preceding the text of the book, but like *Blurbs* if you repurpose an *Epigraph* you don't have to use quotations. They can contain any text you want.

Epigraphs always have a large margin on the top, whether the title is displayed or not. They do not appear in the *Table of Contents*. There's no styling for the heading or the paragraphs.

Below is an example of an *Epigraph*...

> Never trust anyone who has not brought a book with them.
>
> — LEMONY SNICKET

The Foreword Element

The *Foreword Element* is used as an introduction to the work.

Forewords will appear in the *Table of Contents*. They have a large top margin, but if the title is hidden, then the text will appear at the very top. There's no special paragraph styling.

An example of a *Foreword*…

FOREWORD

Here's where I'm introducing this awesome book and telling a little about it.
And the second paragraph of my forward ...

The Introduction Element

An *Introduction* works exactly like the *Foreword*.

The Preface Element

The *Preface* works exactly like the *Foreword*.

The Prologue Element

Prologues occur before the first *Chapter*; typically they are part of the narrative.

Like *Chapters*, the *Prologue Elements* will embellish the heading and paragraphs based on the *Book Style*. *Prologues* appear in the *Table of Contents*.

An example *Prologue*…

PROLOGUE

*I*t would be a long time before a day would go by without Elvis thinking of his mother's death. The doctor said heart attack, but Elvis knew the true story. And even with all the drugs and alcohol in the

The Epilogue Element

An *Epilogue* comes after the last *Chapter*, typically part of the narrative that wraps it up in some way.

Epilogues work exactly like *Prologues*.

The Afterword Element

An *Afterword* is an ending section that often comments in some way about the preceding story.

Afterwords work exactly like *Forewords*.

The Acknowledgements Element

This is where the author of the work acknowledges those who have helped make the work possible.

Acknowledgements work exactly like the *Forewords Element*.

The About the Author Element

About the Author contains a short biography of the author.

About the Author Elements appear in the *Table of Contents*. They have a small top margin and if the heading is hidden, then the text will appear at the very top. There's no styling for the heading or paragraphs.

An interesting feature of *About the Author* is that it contains a box at the bottom of the TEXT EDITOR where you can enter contact details for the author…

Lead-in	For more information:
Webpage	www.example.com
Email	email@example.com
Facebook	Username
Twitter	@handle

This information appears at the bottom of the *About the Author Element* based on the BOOK STYLE as illustrated in the example below…

ABOUT THE AUTHOR

Chuck Heintzelman is an emerging author of action memoirs. This is Chuck's fourth book.
Although he's not sure what happened to his second book.

For more information:

www.example.com
email@example.com

If you enter a Facebook or Twitter value into your *About the Author Element*, it displays as icons in ebooks that are linked to your social account.

Interestingly enough, these icons also display in the print version of your book, but of course there are no links. So in print books I guess they signify that you have a Facebook and/or Twitter account but provide no information on how to get there.

The Also By Element

This *Element* is used to list the author's previously published books. It appears in the *Table of Contents* and has a small top margin. There's no styling for the heading or paragraphs.

All paragraphs are automatically centered in the *Also By Element* unless your BOOK STYLE is set to *Chroma*. In that case all paragraphs are automatically right-justified.

An example of the *Also By Element*...

ALSO BY CHUCK HEINTZELMAN

My First Book

My Third Book

What Happen to My Second Book

The Uncategorized Element

When Vellum cannot determine the type of *Element* while importing a DOCX, it'll make it an *Uncategorized Element*. These *Elements* work exactly the same as *Forewords*.

The Part Element

A *Part* is a structural division that typically groups a set of *Chapters* together. *Parts* appear in the *Table of Contents* and have a Large Top Margin. *Parts* use the HEADING style, but there is no special paragraph styling.

Having text in a *Part Element* is optional and frequently not used.

The following image is an example of a *Part* with text…

PART I

Here's some example text on the *Part Element*. No indent on the first paragraph.

But subsequent paragraphs are indented.

The Volume Element

A *Volume* is used to group other *Elements*. Often *Volumes* are used in bundles or box sets. *Volumes* cannot be grouped in *Part Elements* or within other *Volumes*.

A *Volume* appears in the *Table of Contents* and has a large top margin. The heading of a *Volume* uses the HEADING style from the *BOOK STYLE*, but there is no special paragraph styling.

You can add text on a *Volume*, but frequently *Volumes* do not include any text.

For example…

VOLUME ONE

Creating Parts and Volumes

You can easily create a *Part* or *Volume* by highlighting one or more *Elements* in the *NAVIGATOR* and clicking the gear icon at the bottom of the *NAVIGATOR*...

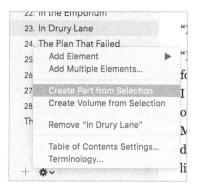

Converting an Element From One Type to Another

To change an *Element* from one type to another, click on the gear icon at the top right of the *TEXT EDITOR* and choose the CONVERT TO > option...

Mr. Teddy Henfrey's First Impressions

At four o'clock, when it was fairly dark and Mrs. Hall was screwing up her courage to go in and ask her visitor if he would take some tea, Teddy Henfrey, the clock-jobber, came into the bar. "My sakes! Mrs. Hall," said he, "but this is terrible weather for thin boots!" The snow outside was falling faster.

Mrs. Hall agreed, and then noticed he had his bag with him. "Now you're here, Mr. Teddy," said she, "I'd be glad if you'd give th' old clock in the parlour a bit of a look. 'Tis going, and it strikes well and hearty; but the hour-hand won't do nuthin' but point at six."

And leading the way, she went across to the parlour door and rapped and entered.

Add Subtitle
Add Heading Image...
Hide Heading in Book

Convert To ▶
✓ Numbered

✓ Chapter

Blurbs
Copyright
Dedication
Epigraph
Foreword
Introduction
Preface
Prologue
Epilogue
Afterword
Acknowledgments
About the Author
Also By

Uncategorized

EIGHT

The Title Page

This chapter explains how and where Vellum builds your book's title page.

The Title Page is Automatically Created

As described in **Chapter 5 – The Title Info**, Vellum automatically creates a *Title Page* based on the values you enter for TITLE, SUBTITLE, AUTHOR, CONTRIBUTORS, PUBLISHER, PUBLISHER LINK, and PUBLISHER LOGO.

There is no way to disable the creation of the *Title Page* in your book.

Below is an example…

THE INVISIBLE MAN

A GROTESQUE ROMANCE

H. G. WELLS

Vellum uses the HEADING style throughout the *Title Page*.

Where is the Title Page Located?

You might think that the *Title Page* appears at the front of your book after the image of the cover on ebooks and as the first page in print books. Most of the time this is true.

Unless your book begins with a *Blurb Element*

Blurbs are special when it comes to the *Title Page*. Vellum places the *Title Page* at the front of your book *after any Blurbs*. If your book begins with multiple *Blurb Elements*, they all are placed before the *Title Page*.

Let's say you have the following *Elements* in your book:

1. *Blurb #1*
2. *Copyright*
3. *Blurb #2*
4. *Introduction*
5. *Chapter 1*

Your book will be created with *Elements* in the following order (*Table of Contents* is ignored in the list below):

1. *Blurb #1*
2. **Title Page**
3. *Copyright*
4. *Blurb #2*
5. *Introduction*
6. *Chapter 1*

Vellum doesn't change the order of your *Elements*, it only adds the *Title Page*. If you moved *Blurb #2* before the *Copyright* so your *NAVIGATOR* has the following in order:

1. *Blurb #1*
2. *Blurb #2*
3. *Copyright*
4. *Introduction*
5. *Chapter 1*

Then Vellum would insert the *Title Page* after *Blurb #2:*

1. *Blurb #1*

2. *Blurb #2*
3. **Title Page**
4. *Copyright*
5. *Introduction*
6. *Chapter 1*

Understanding how this work gives you greater control over the placement of the *Title Page*. If you want several different pages to appear before the *Title Page*, simply have multiple *Blurbs* at the beginning of your book and repurpose them as needed.

Listing Editors on the Title Page

If your book has an editor, illustrator, photographer, or translator, you can enter their names in the Contributors area of the *Title Info* (see **Chapter 5 – The Title Info**). Vellum will list all the contributors on the *Title Page* as illustrated below...

THE INVISIBLE MAN

A GROTESQUE ROMANCE

H. G. WELLS

Edited by

CHUCK HEINTZELMAN

Illustrated by

CHUCK HEINTZELMAN

NINE

Book Styles

This chapter explains the various styling options for your book.

Accessing the Styles

All changes to your book's style are made in the *Book Style* screen. To access the *Book Style* screen click on the Styles tab at the top of the *Navigator*...

This shows you all available styles...

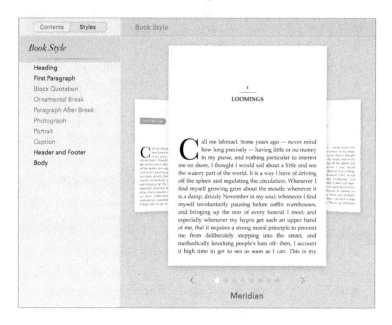

You may have noticed some of the headings in the *Navigator* are bold-faced. This indicates your book is using whatever *Element* or Text Feature that is affected by the style.

Also, Vellum presents a preview of the *Book Style* using the content of your book. If your book doesn't contain content for a particular style, it supplies its own preview.

The Book Style

When have *Book Style* selected at the top of the *Navigator*, you can change the global style for your book. This is illustrated in the previous image.

The *Book Style* window shows a carousel of eight different styles you can select from. Use the arrow keys at the bottom of the carousel to scroll through the options.

Here's a brief overview of each style available:

- *Meridian* – A clean style with strong headings.
- *Trace* – A simple style featuring centered headings with thin fonts.
- *Artisanal* – This style places greater emphasis on headings, using bold fonts and borders above and below the heading.
- *Kindred* – A style featuring fancy flourishes under the headings.
- *Sudo* – A style featuring lightweight, italicized headings.
- *Oxford* – A fancy style with flourishes around the chapter numbers.
- *Parcel* – A style emphasizing the title with thin borders at the top and bottom of the heading's margins.
- *Chroma* – Colored blocks for headings and the text uses spaces between paragraphs instead of indentation. (You can change this with the BODY style, the last item in the NAVIGATOR.)

Remember the *BOOK STYLE* is the overall style settings for the book. You can further customize individual Feature Styles after the *BOOK STYLE* is selected. For example, the HEADING style has three different customizations for the *Meridian Book Style* and six different customizations for the *Chroma Book Style*.

This gives you hundreds of different possible style settings for your book!

Try changing your *BOOK STYLE* and then going into the individual Feature Settings and customizing them until you get your book looking exactly like you want it to look.

Heading Style

The first Feature Style listed in the *NAVIGATOR* is the HEADING style...

Book Style

Heading
First Paragraph
Block Quotation

The HEADING style controls the look of the *Chapter* headings in your book.

First Paragraph Style

Below the HEADING style in the *NAVIGATOR* is the FIRST PARA-GRAPH style. This style controls the look of the first paragraph of normal text in any *Chapter*, *Prologue*, or *Epilogue Elements* in your book.

Each *BOOK STYLE* has between five and seven different variations you can choose from. Drop caps are one of the most used options.

Block Quotation Style

After the FIRST PARAGRAPH style in the *NAVIGATOR* is the BLOCK QUOTATION style. It controls how text with the *Block Quotation* Text Feature is displayed in your book. Each *BOOK STYLE* has three different variations of BLOCK QUOTATION.

Ornamental Break Style

Next up in the *NAVIGATOR* is the ORNAMENTAL BREAK style. *Ornamental Breaks* are a Text Feature most often used as scene breaks in your manuscript. Each *BOOK STYLE* has between six and eight variations of the ORNAMENTAL BREAK style.

Paragraph After Break Style

The next Feature Style in the *NAVIGATOR* is for PARAGRAPHS AFTER BREAK. A "break" is either an *Ornamental Break* or one or more blank paragraphs. This style affects first paragraph after these breaks for only the *Chapter, Prologue,* or *Epilogue Elements* in your book.

Photograph Style

The PHOTOGRAPH style affects all images in your book that you've specified as Photographs. (See **Chapter 14 – Using Images**.)

Each *BOOK STYLE* has five variations of the PHOTOGRAPH style. The various options place different styles of borders and shadows around the Photographs.

———

Shadows around images only
appear in ebooks, not print books.

———

Portrait Style

The PORTRAIT style is used on all images in your book that you've indicated are Portraits. Each BOOK STYLE has four variations.

Caption Style

Vellum allows you to add a caption to any *Inline Image* within your book. The CAPTION style determines how this caption is displayed. Each *BOOK STYLE* has five variations.

Header and Footer Style

The HEADER AND FOOTER style only affects print books. The style specifies the position of page numbers, the author's name, the book's title, and the chapter's title. Each *BOOK STYLE* has eight different variations.

Browse through each variation to make sure your print book appears exactly how you want it to appear.

Resetting the Book Style

As you're exploring all the possible style options, it's easy to lose track of changes. Sometimes you want to reset the styles to defaults.

Vellum provides a small indicator at the top right of the Style Pane that indicates the style settings are not the default for the current *BOOK STYLE*...

If that little reset indicator is visible, it means something has changed from default and clicking on it will reset the style to defaults.

If *BOOK STYLE* is selected when you click on the indicator, all Feature Styles for the currently selected *BOOK STYLE* (Meridian, Oxford, etc.) will be reset. But if you have a Feature Style selected in the *NAVIGATOR*, only that Feature will be reset.

Body Style

The last Feature Style in the *NAVIGATOR* is the BODY style. It's not really a "Feature" style because it does not apply to just one feature, but instead affects the text for your entire book. When you select *BOOK STYLE* from the *NAVIGATOR*, you'll see the following screen...

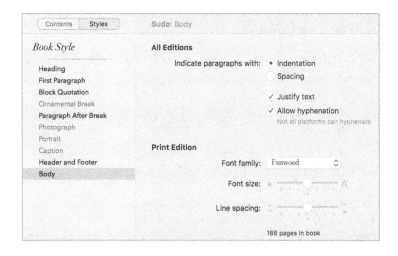

The paragraph, justification, and hyphenation settings affect both ebooks and print books. The font family, font size, and line spacing apply only to print books.

The options for BODY style are the same, regardless of *BOOK STYLE*. But when you change *BOOK STYLES*, any changes you made do not transfer to the newly selected *BOOK STYLE*. Make it a practice to *always* review each Feature Style and the BODY style after changing your *BOOK STYLE*. (This can save frustration later.)

Ebook Fonts

You have some control over the print font by changing it in the BODY style settings explained in the last section. But you have no control over the fonts used in ebooks. Since ereaders allow the reader to select their font, unless they're using the *Publisher* or *Original* font, they won't see how cool the fonts are in your ebook.

Vellum will embed certain fonts within the ebook, the non-standard ones, so they can be used on most ereaders.

The rest of this chapter lists the major fonts used in the ebooks produced for each *BOOK STYLE*. You can Google the fonts listed for more details about a particular font.

Meridian Book Style

- Body – Palantino
- Headings – Palantino
- Drop caps – Baskerville

Trace Book Style

- Body – Palantino
- Headings – Quicksand (embedded)
- Drop caps – Baskerville

Artisanal Book Style

- Body – Palantino
- Headings – League Gothic (embedded) and Great Vibes (embedded)
- Drop caps – Baskerville or Great Vibes (embedded)

Kindred Book Style

- Body – Palantino and Alegreya (embedded)
- Headings – Alegreya (embedded)
- Drop caps – Great Vibes (embedded)

Sudo Book Style

- Body – Palantino
- Headings – Lekton (embedded)
- Drop caps – Baskerville

Oxford Book Style

- Body – Palantino
- Headings – IM Fell Double Pica PRO (embedded)
- Drop caps – IM Fell Double Pica PRO (embedded)

Parcel Book Style

- Body – Palantino
- Headings – Josefin Sans (embedded)
- Drop caps – Baskerville

Chroma Book Style

- Body – Palantino

- Headings – Quicksand (embedded)
- Drop caps – Baskerville

TEN

Preview

_____

This chapter explains how to use Vellum's Preview.

About Vellum's Preview

Vellum's *PREVIEW* feature provides a live preview of how your book will appear across a variety of devices. You can also see what the print book will look like. The *PREVIEW* appears along the right portion of the Vellum application...

If *PREVIEW* is not visible, click the **PREVIEW** button in the *TOP BAR* to toggle the display...

The *PREVIEW* shows what your book will be rendered as on the device or paper. The example below is the *Title Page* on a Kindle Fire…

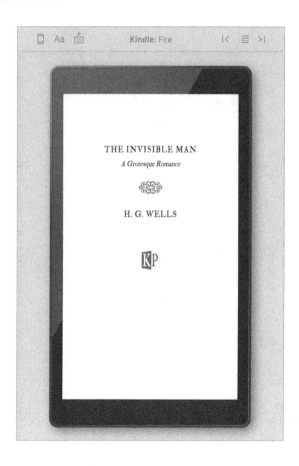

Changing the Previewed Device

Clicking on the left most icon at the top of *PREVIEW* will pop up a menu allowing you to change the device displayed in the *PREVIEW*...

As you can see in the above image, there are seven different devices on which you can preview your ebook, as well as a PRINT option to see what your paper book looks like.

The Device Settings Menu

The second icon on the TOP BAR will bring up the DEVICE SETTINGS menu...

Changing the DEVICE SETTINGS allows you to evaluate how a reader will see your book if they change the font size, font face, or if they switch to a different viewing mode.

Keep in mind these settings do not affect your book in any way. They are simply changing how you are previewing the book.

When you're previewing print books, the DEVICE SETTINGS gives you two options...

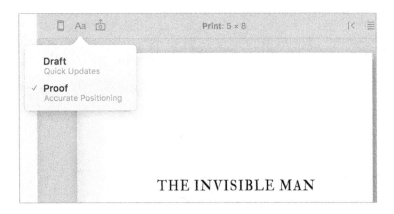

DRAFT mode is quicker, but may not show an accurate representation of what your print book will look like. For example, Vellum automatically fixes Widows (the last line of a paragraph appearing at the top of a page) but those may not be fixed in DRAFT mode.

PROOF mode is much more processor intensive. It is best to use DRAFT mode if you are making significant changes to your book.

In PROOF mode, you will see each page with the automatic layout changes Vellum performs. See **Chapter 17 – Creating Print Books** for more details. There's also subtle shading on the left or right edge of your pages. You know when the shade is on the left edge of the page, you are viewing a page what will appear on the right side of the your book. And vice versa.

Navigating the Preview

The icons on the top of *PREVIEW*, on the right, allow you to navigate through your book.

The buttons will 1) move to the previous chapter, 2) show the *Table of Contents*, or 3) move to the next chapter. The image below illustrates the middle button being clicked…

To move back or forward a page at a time, click on the left or right edge of the page previewed.

ELEVEN

Page Numbers

This chapter explains how Vellum generates page numbers for print books.

Two Types of Page Numbers

When you create print books, Vellum uses two types of page numbers. It uses lowercase Roman numbers (iv., v., vi.) for pages in the front matter of the book and normal integers after the front matter.

Below is an example page from a print book with lower-case Roman numbers...

> bered holding the candle while Mrs. Hall shot these bolts overnight. At the sight he stopped, gaping, then with the bottle still in his hand went upstairs again. He rapped at the
>
> *xiii*

So how does Vellum determine where the standard, integer numbering begins? Easy. Vellum goes through your book's

Elements in order and the first *Element* not listed below will start normal numbering.

- *Copyright*
- *Dedication*
- *Epigraph*
- *Foreword*
- *Introduction*
- *Preface*
- *Afterword (yeah, weird, but Afterwords don't trigger normal numbering)*
- *Acknowledgements*
- *About the Author*
- *Also By*

————

You don't really need to worry about page numbers.

It all happens automatically.

But if you want to know why numbers are appearing a certain way, you can carefully review the first *Elements* in your book and compare them to the list above.

————

Which Elements Show Page Numbers?

Although the number of every page in your print book is tracked, whether it's using small Roman numbers or normal integers, not every *Element* displays page numbers.

Elements that DO display page numbers

Foreword, Introduction, Preface, Prologue, Epilogue, Afterword and *Chapter.*

Elements that DON'T display page numbers

Blurbs, Copyright, Dedication, Epigraph, Acknowledgements, About the Author, Also By, and *Uncategorized.*

TWELVE

Table of Contents

This chapter explains how Vellum generates the Table of Contents.

Where is the Table of Contents Located?

L ike the *Title Page*, the *Table of Contents* is automatically placed in your book. You can change this, which is explained a bit later in this chapter.

Where the *Table of Contents* appears within the book varies. It depends on the *Elements* at the beginning of your book.

There are four special *Elements* that can come before the *Table of Contents*. These are the same four *Elements* listed in the chart back at the beginning of **Chapter 7 – Vellum Elements** as not displaying in the *Table of Contents*:

1. *Blurb*
2. *Copyright*
3. *Dedication*
4. *Epigraph*

Thus, the *Table of Contents*, if used, will immediately proceed the first *Element* in your book not in the above list.

Ebooks Can Have Two Tables of Contents

Ebooks always have a Logical Table of Contents. This is part of how ebooks are organized internally. When a reader views the Table of Contents using their device's navigation controls, they are viewing this Logical Table of Contents.

But an ebook can also have a *Table of Contents* that is a part of the book itself. Like a *Chapter or Copyright*, this *Table of Contents* appears as part of the book's content.

Table of Contents Settings

To change the behavior of *Table of Contents* generation in your book, you need to access the *Table of Contents Settings*. You can do this by clicking the gear icon at the bottom of the *Navigator*...

This presents you with the *Table of Contents Settings*...

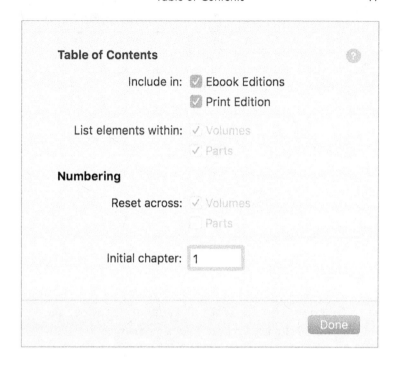

Here you can select whether the *Table of Contents* shows in your ebook and print versions. You can also specify the initial chapter number of your book.

If your book contains *Volumes* or *Parts,* you can select whether or not to list their items in the *Table of Contents*. This is often useful if you have a large book or box set.

You can also control if chapter numbering is reset across *Volumes* and *Parts*. The default is to reset the numbering on each *Volume* since *Volumes* are often complete works by themselves, but to not reset across *Parts* since they are portions of a larger work.

Why the Table of Contents is Always at the Front

The standard Table of Contents position in print books has always been near the front. But an ebook is a different can of worms.

Up until a couple years ago, authors would often place their Table of Contents at the back of the book, the idea being it wouldn't take up valuable space when readers sample the book. In fact, past versions of Vellum allowed you to specify whether the Table of Contents appeared at the front or back of your ebook.

But Amazon stopped allowing the Table of Contents to appear at the back.

> Putting a book's Table of Contents (TOC) at the end of the book can create a poor experience for readers... if the formatting of a book results in a poor experience or genuine reader confusion, or is designed to unnaturally inflate sales or pages read, we will take action to remove titles and protect readers.
>
> Kindle Direct Publishing Announcement, March 14, 2016

So now Vellum only allows the *Table of Contents* to appear towards the front.

My belief is the *real* reason Amazon changed this policy is that ebooks with contents at the back showed as not completely read. A reader would get to the end of the story and stop reading, not clicking past those final few pages of the ebook. But who knows? Maybe reader confusion played a part in their decision.

Contents Terminology

You can change a few of the terms used in the structure of your book. For instance, let's say instead of "Part" you want *Parts* to show as "Section." To access the CONTENTS TERMI-NOLOGY click on the gear at the bottom of the NAVIGATOR...

This will show you the CONTENTS TERMINOLOGY...

Contents Terminology

Title Page | Title Page

Chapter | Chapter

Part | Part

Volume | Volume

Done

Changing these terms will change the usage both in the *NAVI-GATOR* and the *Table of Contents*.

An Example

Your *BOOK STYLE* is applied to the *Table of Contents*. There are no special flourishes as those that can appear on *Chapter Elements*, but the fonts are matched to the rest of your book.

Follows is a portion of the *Table of Contents* for a print book…

CONTENTS

About the Author   xi
Also by H. G. Wells   xiii
Preface   xv

1. The Strange Man's Arrival   1
2. Mr. Teddy Henfrey's First Impressions   8
3. The Thousand and One Bottles   13

THIRTEEN

Text Features

This chapter explains the various Text Features available within Vellum.

What are Text Features?

T ext Features are special formatting options for your text. Some Text Features are applied automatically when you import a DOCX into Vellum. Other Text Features can be applied automatically if you use Vellum's Custom Styles in the Word DOCX you import.

But you can always edit your content in the TEXT EDITOR to add any desired Text Features.

Many Text Features appear differently based on your BOOK STYLE.

Accessing the Text Features Menu

You can access the TEXT FEATURES menu by clicking on the asterisk (*) icon at the top left of the TEXT EDITOR.

You'll see an image similar to the following...

Subheads

Subheads allow you to add subheadings within your text. When you choose SUBHEAD from the *TEXT FEATURES* menu, you can then enter the text for the subheading...

The subheading's appearance within your book is based on your *BOOK STYLE*...

An Example Subhead

The stranger came early in February, one wintry day,

Ornamental Breaks

As described in **Chapter 4 – Importing Your Manuscript**, Vellum is pretty good at detecting and applying the *Ornament Break* Text Feature when it discovers them in the DOCX you're importing. But you can also use the *TEXT FEATURES* menu to insert them into the *TEXT EDITOR*.

They'll appear as three asterisks (* * *) in your *TEXT EDITOR*...

---

the table, he took up his quarters in the inn.

* * *

Mrs. Hall lit the fire and left him there while she went to

But how they appear in your book depends on the *BOOK STYLE*...

---

quarters in the inn.

∼

Mrs. Hall lit the fire and left him there while she went to

Images

Selecting IMAGE from the *TEXT FEATURES* menu allows you to insert images into the *TEXT EDITOR*. Images are covered in more detail in **Chapter 14 – Using Images**.

Alignment Blocks

When you select a chunk of text in the *TEXT EDITOR* and then choose ALIGNMENT BLOCK from the *TEXT FEATURES* menu, the text you selected will become center aligned and have large square brackets on each side of the block…

> The stranger came early in February, one wintry day,
> through a biting wind and a driving snow, …|

The large square brackets only appear when your cursor is on text within the block.

Notice that little gear icon at the top right of the Alignment Block? You can use this to change the justification from CENTER to LEFT or RIGHT. You can also use the gear icon to clear the *Alignment Block*, reverting it back to normal text…

Lists

Vellum supports both bulleted and numbered lists. Select one or more lines of text and then choose LIST from the *TEXT*

FEATURES menu and Vellum will turn the items into a bulleted list…

If you choose LIST from the Text Features Menu without first selecting text, a new *List* will be inserted at your cursor's position and you can begin typing the list.

Use the gear icon at the top right of the List to change to a numbered list or to clear the formatting…

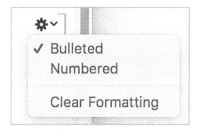

Block Quotation

Same process with *Block Quotations*—either select a portion of text first or let Vellum insert the *Block Quotation* block at your cursor's position…

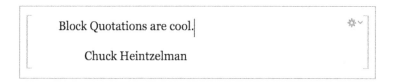

Use the gear icon to add an attribution to the quote, or remove the formatting…

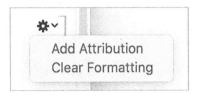

Verses

Verses work the same way as *Block Quotations*, as far as applying them and adding attributions. The styling for *Verses* uses italicized text with hanging indents…

> *Roses are red,*
> *Violets are blue,*
> *Some poems rhyme,*
> *But the last line of this poem really screwed*
> *   that up.*

Web Links

Web Links apply only to ebooks. They allow you to add a link to a web page. Just highlight the text you want to make a link, and choose WEB LINK from the *TEXT FEATURES* menu…

This brings up the WEB LINK box. *Web Links* appear in the TEXT EDITOR as blue text.

Any time you click on a *Web Link* in the TEXT EDITOR, the WEB LINK box will pop up so you can edit or remove the link.

———

Do Not Add Underlines to Indicate Web Links

Vellum does this for you based on the BOOK STYLE. And obviously the print version cannot have links. It looks amateurish to have a print book with underlined web addresses.

———

Store Links

Store Links are one of the coolest Vellum features. They allow you to specify link to your ebook's product page on the various platforms Vellum generates ebooks for. Thus the Kindle-specific version of your ebook has links to Amazon, but the Kobo-specific version of your ebook links to Kobo.

Create *Store Links* the same way as you create *Web Links*, except choose STORE LINK from the *TEXT FEATURES* menu. This will bring up the *STORE LINK* box as illustrated below…

Here you can enter the store identifiers for each platform you're generating ebooks on. If you're only generating for Kindle and Kobo, you'd only see the KINDLE and KOBO slots in the box.

Use the **SELECT PLATFORMS…** button to add or remove the platforms you're generating ebooks on.

If you don't have the store identifier for one of the platforms, leave it blank. The ebook version generated for that platform won't have a link.

Affiliate Codes

If you go into Vellum's preferences (choose VELLUM > PREFER-
ENCES... from the menu), you can set up the affiliate codes
Vellum will use when creating *Store Links*...

FOURTEEN

Using Images

This chapter discusses using images in Vellum.

Two Types of Images

Besides the cover image, which was discussed in **Chapter 5 – The Ebook Cover**, there are two types of images you can add to your books: *Heading Images* and *Inline Images*.

A *Heading Image* is always associated with the heading of an *Element*. *Inline Images* can be placed on any *Element* anywhere within the text of the *Element*.

Adding a Heading Image

To add a Heading Image to an *Element*, click the gear icon at the top right of the *Text Editor*...

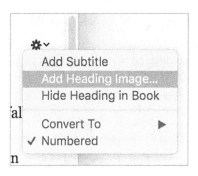

This will allow you to select an image to add to the heading. When you add the image, it shows to the left of the *Element's* heading in the TEXT EDITOR...

If there's an issue with the image, you'll see a small warning icon in the image. Click the image to discover what the error is...

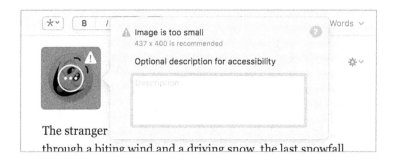

In the above example, the problem is that the image is too small. You can use the gear icon again to replace the image with one the correct size.

———

Heading Images must be at least 400 pixels on the shortest side.

———

Heading Images display below the heading in your ebooks or print book as the following example shows…

THE STRANGE MAN'S ARRIVAL

*T*he stranger came early in February, one wintry day, through a biting wind and a driving snow,

Adding Multiple Heading Images

Keep in mind that adding images to your book increases the size of your ebooks. If you add the same *Heading Image* to multiple *Elements*, your ebook will actually have multiple copies of this same image.

A better way to add a *Heading Image* to multiple *Elements* is to select multiple *Elements* in the *Navigator* (hold ALT+CMD and click on each desired ELEMENT to do this) and then select CHAPTER > HEADING > ADD HEADING IMAGE... from the menu.

The image below illustrates this...

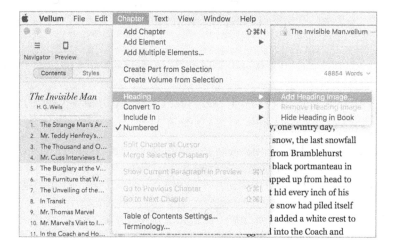

This will add the same Heading Image to each selected *Element*, but only store the image once in your ebook, thus saving space.

Inline Images

There are two ways to add *Inline Images* to an *Element*. You can use the Text Features menu and select IMAGE, which prompts you for the image and inserts it at the cursor's current location in the *TEXT EDITOR*. Or you can drag and drop an image from Finder to the Text Edit.

Either way, and you'll have an *Inline Image* block in the *TEXT EDITOR*...

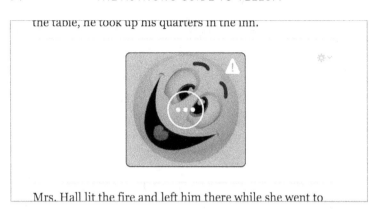

The gear icon in the *Inline Image* block allows you to replace the image or add a caption to the image.

When you click on the image, you'll get a pop up with a few more details than the *Heading Image* has…

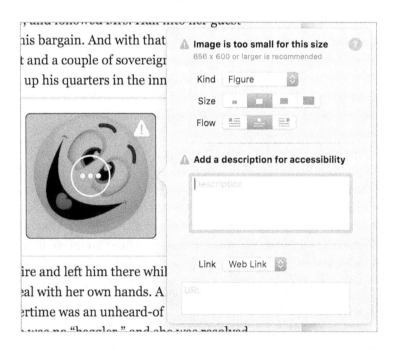

Image Kind

You can select from five different image kinds:

1. *Photograph* – these images will be styled according to the PHOTOGRAPH style from the *BOOK STYLE*.
2. *Figure* – figures will have a small gray border around the image. Useful for charts and other graphics.
3. *Portrait* – these images will be styled according to the PORTRAIT style from the *BOOK STYLE*.
4. *Freestanding* – does not style the image.
5. *Book Cover* – these images are styled with a shadow on ebooks. (Remember that print books never receive shadow effects on images.)

Size

You can specify four sizes for your image:

1. *Small* – Uses 35% of the device or page width.
2. *Medium* – Uses 50% of the device or page width.
3. *Large* – Uses 75% of the device or page width.
4. *Full* – Uses 100% of the device or page width.

———

When the image's height is taller than the device or page height, it is always resized to fit within the page and the aspect ratio is maintained. This means if you have a very tall image, it may not use the width you expect based on the SIZE setting.

———

Flow

If you set the SIZE setting to either *Small* or *Medium,* you can also set how the text flows around the image.

Description

You should always add descriptions to images. This assists blind or vision-impaired readers.

Link

Optionally you can have the image go to either a *Web Link* or a *Store Link.*

Image Dimension Requirements

As mentioned earlier, *Heading Images* must be 400 pixels long on the shortest side.

Inline Images have different requirements based on the SIZE setting for the image. The list below details each size:

- *Small* – must be at least 460 pixels wide.
- *Medium* – must be at least 656 pixels wide.
- *Large* – must be at least 984 pixels wide.
- *Full* – must be at least 1,312 pixels wide.

———

Always Use 300 DPI for Images

If you are going to generate print books, make sure all images are at least 300 DPI.

(This will save you from frustration later.)

FIFTEEN

Exporting to RTF

———————————

This chapter discusses Vellum's Export to RTF feature.

How to Export to a RTF

Vellum gives you the ability to export your book to a RTF file, which is a standard format readable by a vast majority of word processors.

To do this, simply choose FILE > EXPORT TO RTF... from the menu, enter a filename, and click the **SAVE** button...

🍎	**Vellum**	File	Edit	Chapter	Text

New	⌘N
Open...	⌘O
Open Recent	▶
Import Word File...	
Close	⌘W
Save	⌘S
Duplicate	⇧⌘S
Rename...	
Move To...	
Revert To	▶
Reimport Word File...	
Generate Books...	⇧⌘B
Export to RTF...	
Select Platforms...	
Print Settings...	⇧⌘P

Navigator   Preview

Contents

The Invisible
H. G. Wells

1. The Strange
2. Mr. Teddy He
3. The Thousan
4. Mr. Cuss Inte
5. The Burglary
6. The Furniture
7. The Unveilin
8. In Transit

How Each Feature is Exported

The resulting RTF is clean; the text formatting is exported cleanly. The only thing missing in the RTF will be your book's images (both *Heading Images* and *Inline Images*).

Here's a breakdown of how each element is exported:

- *Element Headings* – They start a new page and are centered on the page. The font used is Helvetica 18pt bold.
- *Heading Images* – These images do not appear in the RTF.
- *Element Subtitles* – They are centered under the heading using the Helvetica 12pt font.

- *Subheads* – Subheadings end up Helvetica 14pt bold and are left justified.
- *Paragraphs* – Paragraphs are left justified and the first line is indented.
- *Ornamental Breaks* – These are replaced with three asterisks (* * *) and centered on a line by themselves.
- *Inline Images* – These appear in the RTF as the image file's name in square brackets. For example: [Image: filename.jpg]. The font used is Courier 10 pt. If the image has a caption, it is centered under the file's name in Helvetica 10pt.
- *Lists* – Both numeric and bulleted lists appear fine in the resulting RTF.
- *Block Quotes and Verses* – Both of these Text Features have 1-inch margins on either side. Any *Attribution* will have a 2½-inch margin on the left.
- *Web Links* – There is no special styling assigned to *Web Links*. They appear as normal text. But if you find the link, you can edit it.
- *Store Links* – These come through as *Web Links* using the first linked store. The website is actually Vellum's redirector service for *Store Links* in your ebooks.

Converting the RTF to DOCX

You can use Microsoft Word to convert the RTF to a DOCX. Just open up the RTF with Word and then choose FILE > CONVERT DOCUMENT from the menu…

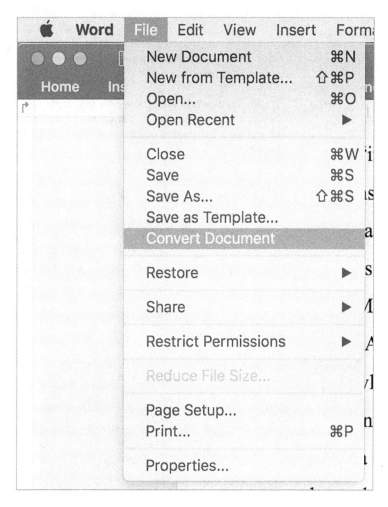

When you select this option, you'll receive a warning message…

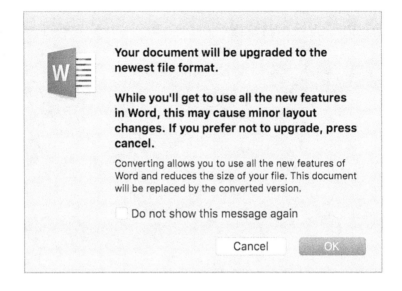

Once you press the **OK** button, the document will be in DOCX format and you can save it.

Importing the DOCX

If you proceed to import the converted DOCX back into Vellum, there's a few discrepancies you'll have to fix:

- *Heading Subtitles* – These will appear as normal text at the top of the *Element* with an *Alignment Block* centering them.
- *Subheads* – These will become bold-faced paragraphs.
- *Inline Images* – The [Image: filename.jpg] and any caption will come through as normal text, centered in an *Alignment Block*. You'll need to reinsert every image.
- *Lists* – These come through as normal text, each item a new paragraph.

- *Block Quotes and Verses* – These will appear as normal text, with attributions as a new paragraph.
- *Store Links* – There will be no *Store Links* because the export converted them into *Web Links*.

What's the Point?

The point of this entire chapter is that, although technically it's possible to export your manuscript, make some changes, and then import the converted DOCX, it is far easier not to.

You'll spend a lot of time tweaking everything once you get back into Vellum.

The best workflow is to only use Vellum as your publishing platform, and always go back to your original DOCX if you need to make significant changes. Especially if you're using Vellum Custom Styles as explained in **Chapter 4 – Importing Your Manuscript**.

But, if you're just fixing a quick typo or two, the fastest way to accomplish this is to update both your original DOCX (think of this as your integrity copy) and your Vellum file (within the *Text Editor*). And then, if needed, **Generate** your books again.

SIXTEEN

Generating Ebooks

This chapter explains the process for generating ebooks.

Deciding What to Generate

The first step to generating your ebooks is to click the **GENERATE** button at the right edge of the *TOP BAR*...

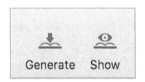

This will show the *GENERATE SCREEN*...

TIP

Always look for your book's cover along the left edge of the
Generate Screen. If missing, it's a reminder you haven't
added your ebook cover yet.

Select Platforms

Click on the (**...**) button across from Generate for: to select
the platforms for generation…

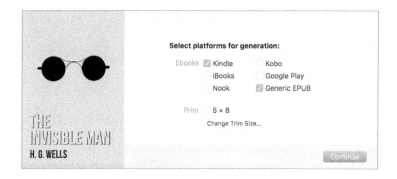

Once you check the Ebooks you would like to generate for, click the **Continue** button to go back to the *Generate Screen*.

Click the Generate Button

From the *Generate Screen*, click the **Generate** button when you're ready to create the ebooks.

When you do this, a spinner will start twirling while Vellum goes through each platform you selected. This is when it CREATES BEAUTIFUL EBOOKS, ready for you to upload to the various stores.

If you click the **Show Files** button from the *Generation Complete Screen* (or the **Show** button at the right on your *Top Bar*), Finder will open listing the files you generated...

Name	^	Date Modified
▼ Generic EPUB		Today, 7:35 PM
The-Invisible-Man-Generic.epub		Today, 7:35 PM
The-Invisible-Man-Generic.jpg		Today, 7:09 PM
▼ Kindle		Today, 7:35 PM
The-Invisible-Man-Kindle.jpg		Today, 7:09 PM
The-Invisible-Man-Kindle.mobi		Today, 7:35 PM

Where to Upload Your Ebooks

Part of the power of Vellum is that it creates different ebooks for each major platform. Each ebook is optimized for the specific platform, handling all the idiosyncrasies for you.

Your ebooks will just work, regardless of where your readers download them.

Kindle

The files in the KINDLE folder allow you to publish your ebook on Amazon through their Kindle Direct Publishing service. Upload the MOBI file from this directory for the book's content file and the JPG file for the cover.

iBooks

The iBOOKS folder contains the files you'll need to sell your ebook on the iBooks store. To do this, you'll need to run an OS X app called iTunes Producer. Drag the JPG from the folder to the COVER ART section of iTunes Producer. And from the FILES tab of iTunes Producer, drag the EPUB file to where it says "DRAG YOUR FULL BOOK HERE."

Nook

The files in the NOOK folder allow you to publish your ebook at Barnes & Noble using their Nook Press service. Choose the EPUB file when you need to UPLOAD MANUSCRIPT FILE. Then from the COVER IMAGE side tab, click CHOOSE A FILE TO UPLOAD and use the JPG file. (When Nook Press asks if you want to add the cover to your manuscript, answer No.)

Kobo

In the KOBO folder, you'll have the files needed to publish your ebook at Kobo using their Kobo Writing Life service. Use the JPG file when you click the big UPLOAD YOUR BOOK COVER image. On the ADD EBOOK CONTENT SCREEN, choose the generated EPUB file and click the **UPLOAD** button.

Google Play

The files in the GOOGLE PLAY folder allow you to publish your ebook at Google Play using their Google Play Books Partner Center. From the CONTENT tab, upload both the EPUB and JPG and they'll process them accordingly.

Generic EPUB

The GENERIC EPUB folder contains a JPG and EPUB that you can use to upload to aggregators such as Smashwords or Draft2Digital. You could also upload these files to that awesome book bundling service BundleRabbit (although BundleRabbit allows you to upload your Vellum file for greater flexibility).

SEVENTEEN

Creating Print Books

This chapter explains the process of creating print books.

Print Settings

O ne of the first things you'll want to do when creating print books is to review your PRINT SETTINGS. To access PRINT SETTINGS, select FILE > PRINT SETTINGS… from Vellum's menu…

This will present you with the *PRINT SETTINGS* box...

Print Settings

Trim Size:

5 × 8   5¼ × 8   5½ × 8½   6 × 9

Inside Margin:

0.875 in   ⌄

● First chapter begins on right side
○ Every chapter begins on right side

Include Images In:
● Black & White
○ Color

178 pages in book   Done

The *PRINT SETTINGS* box has a number of options.

Trim Size

You have four different trim sizes you can choose from. When you change the trim size, Vellum changes the outside margin and the font size, and recalculates the number of pages in your book.

Inside Margin

This specifies the size of the margin closest to the book's spine. Vellum sets a sensible default for you, but you may have to adjust this depending on the size of your book and the paper you'll be using to print the book.

CreateSpace has the following minimum requirements for the inside margin:

- 24 to 150 pages – minimum inside margin is **.375"**
- 151 to 400 pages – minimum inside margin is **.75"**
- 401 to 600 pages – minimum inside margin is **.875"**
- more than 600 pages – minimum inside margin is **1.0"**

Keep in mind these are minimums! To my taste, having a margin ¼ to ½ an inch greater than these minimums makes the book easier to read.

Where Each Chapter Begins

Here you decide if only the first *Chapter* in your book begins on the right side of the printed book, or if every *Chapter* begins on the right side. Vellum inserts blank pages when needed to force a page to the right side.

Specifically, if you select FIRST CHAPTER BEGINS ON RIGHT SIDE, then only *Chapters* and *Epilogues* could appear on the left side, and then only when they follow a *Chapter.* Otherwise, *Chapters* and *Epilogues* will always begin on the right side of the book.

The *Elements* that always begin on the right side of the book regardless of this setting are

- *Title Page*
- *Table of Contents*
- *Dedication*
- *Epigraph*
- *Foreword*
- *Introduction*
- *Preface*
- *Afterword*
- *Acknowledgements*
- *About the Author*
- *Also By*

Copyrights and *Blurbs* can start on the left side of the printed book, no matter what your selection of CHAPTER BEGINS is set to.

Include Images in

Here you specify if images should be converted to black and white in your print book. Or if they should remain in color.

———

Don't forget, images in your book must be at least 300 dpi for print books.

———

Other Settings Affecting Print

There are two other areas where the settings affect your print books.

Table of Contents

The TABLE OF CONTENTS SETTINGS was discussed in **Chapter 12 – Table of Contents**. There you can specify whether to generate a *Table of Contents* for print books and whether to include details from *Volumes* and *Parts* in the *Table of Contents*.

Book Style Settings

Besides the overall BOOK STYLE you're using, you'll want to review the HEADER AND FOOTER style for your print book. And don't forget the BODY style because there you can set the FONT FAMILY, FONT SIZE, and LINE SPACING.

Generating the Print File

Click the **GENERATE** button in the TOP BAR to get to the GENERATE SCREEN...

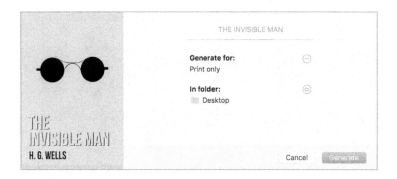

You can click the (**...**) button across from GENERATE FOR if you need to enable generation for print books, or if you want to change the trim size.

Once you're ready to create your print file click the **Generate** button.

This will create a PDF file in a Print folder, down from the folder you specified on the *Generate Screen*.

You now have an interior PDF of your book, suitable for use with print services such as CreateSpace, IngramSpark, and Nook Press.

Widows and Orphans

One of the most time-consuming editing tasks when creating a print book is handling widows and orphans.

Widows occur when the last line of a paragraph is left dangling at the top of a page…

14 | THE INVISIBLE MAN

his whip.

They saw the dog's teeth had slipped the hand, heard a kick, saw the dog execute a flanking jump and get home on the stranger's leg, and heard the rip of his trousering. Then the finer end of Fearenside's whip reached his property, and the dog, yelping with dismay, retreated under the wheels of the waggon. It was all the business of a swift half-minute. No one spoke, everyone shouted. The stranger

Since widows look a little hinky on the page, Vellum automatically fixes them by moving a line from the bottom of the previous page to fix it.

Orphans are basically the opposite the opposite of widows. They are when only the first line of a paragraph appears at the bottom of a page.

Vellum does not fix orphans. Their help page states:

Unlike a widow, an orphan is left in place by Vellum. This practice conforms with modern typesetting standards.

Balancing Spreads

As Vellum creates your PDF, it makes sure the text at the bottom of each two-page spread is aligned evenly. If Vellum didn't do this, then when it fixed widows the result would be an "unbalanced spread"…

"That I think, is all," said the stranger, with that quietly irresistible air of finality he could assume at will. Mrs. Hall reserved her question and sympathy for a better occasion.

After Mrs. Hall had left the room, he remained standing in front of the fire, glaring, so Mr. Henfrey puts it, at the clock-mending. Mr. Henfrey not only took off the hands of the clock, and the face, but extracted the works; and he tried to work in as slow and quiet and

couldn't be more wrapped and bandaged."

At Gleeson's corner he saw Hall, who had recently married the stranger's hostess at the Coach and Horses, and who now drove the Iping conveyance, when occasional people required it, to Sidderbridge Junction, coming towards him on his return from that place. Hall had evidently been "stopping a bit" at Sidderbridge, to judge by his driving. "Ow do, Teddy?" he said, passing.

"You got a rum un up home!" said Teddy.

Although, if Vellum cannot balance the spread when fixing a widow, it will leave the widow in place.

Figuring your Book's Spine Thickness

When you use a print service to create your print book, you'll need to create a cover for your book. Since the cover includes the front page, back page, and the spine, you'll need to determine how thick your spine is.

For CreateSpace, this is easy. First determine the number of pages in your print book. (You can find the number of pages on the *Print Settings* screen discussed at the beginning of this chapter.) And then use the correct formula below:

- *Color interior books:* **Page count x 0.002347**

- *Black and white interior with white paper:* **Page count x
  0.002252**
- *Black and white interior with cream paper:* **Page count x
  0.0025**

A 172-page book, black and white interior with white paper
would be 172 x 0.002252 = 0.387"

The formulas for figuring the dimensions of your cover are

Width
Trim width x 2 + Spine width + 0.25

Height
Trim height x 2 + 0.25

So at CreateSpace, a 172-page book using black and white
images on white paper having a trim of 6" x 9" would be
12.637" wide by 18.25" high. (This includes the 0.125" bleed.)

EIGHTEEN

Creating Ebook Box Sets

This chapter explains how to create box sets with Vellum.

What is a Box Set?

The terms "boxset," "box set," or "boxed set" all refer to multi-volume ebooks, usually containing a variety of works. Although "boxed set" is the most grammatically correct way to refer this type of collection, "box set" seems to be the prevalent usage.

Sometimes you'll see an image that is a 3D representation of what the box set would look like if it were a physical box set...

Although these types of images look pretty cool and illustrate the multi-volume nature of box sets, don't use them as the cover image for retailers such as Kobo, Amazon, and iTunes. There are two reasons for this.

First, some vendors (such as iBooks) do not accept 3D images for an ebook cover. They fear that when a customer sees a 3D image, they'll expect to get a physical box set, not an electronic version.

The second reason is that the space Kobo, Amazon, etc., allocates to display an ebook's cover is optimized for single books, not box sets. The 3D image will be smaller and there will be wasted white space...

As you can see, you lose almost half of your cover space.

The Steps to Building Your Box Set

Here are the steps to create a box set:

1. *Prep work* – Where you get everything ready.
2. *The Title Info* – Entering the title, author, and publisher info.
3. *The cover* – Adding the cover image to Vellum.
4. *Create a skeleton* – Add the front matter, back matter, and a bunch of placeholder *Chapters*.
5. *Dragging and dropping* – Dragging the Vellum files for each volume into the box set.
6. *Cleanup* – Removing placeholder *Chapters*, checking the *Table of Contents*, and tweaking the BOOK STYLE.
7. *Ebook generation* – Clicking the **GENERATE** button.

This may sound like a lot of steps, but it goes quickly.

The rest of this chapter explains each step in greater detail.

Step 1 - Prep Work

A cover image for the box set needs to be created. This image will be part of the ebook and is used to advertise the box set at Kobo, Amazon, iBooks, etc.

Each ebook you'll be adding to the box set needs to be in a separate Vellum file. You could import multiple DOCX files into Vellum (using the drag and drop technique we'll be using with the Vellum files), but building the box set with Vellum files requires less tweaking of each *Volume* in your box set.

Once you have the cover images, and all the ebooks as Vellum files, the entire process of building a box set takes less then 10 minutes.

Step 2 - Title Info

Create a new file in Vellum, and then enter all the *Title Info...*

| Title Info | Ebook Cover |

Title | The Not Only Humans Bundle

Subtitle | Twelve Ebook Box Set

Author | Leah | Middle | Cutter

Contributors

Author | Douglas | Middle | Smith

Author | Blaze | Middle | Ward

Author | Kim | Middle | Antieau

Author | Mindy | Middle | Klasky

Author | Anthea | Middle | Sharp

Publisher | Kydala Publishing, Inc.

Publisher Link | bundlerabbit.com

Publisher Logo | Image satisfies size requirements

Language | English

Ebook ISBN | Optional

The *TITLE INFO* is explained in greater detail in **Chapter 5 – The Title Info**.

Step 3 - The Cover

Following the instructions from **Chapter 6 – The Ebook Cover**, attach your cover image to your box set.

Step 4 - Create a Skeleton

In this step, you create a number of *Elements* in the *Navigator*. Add any *Elements* for the book's front matter and back matter, and then create a bunch of blank *Chapters* in the middle of the book. I call these placeholder *Chapters*. The reason to use placeholder *Chapters* is that it's easier to drag and drop a Vellum file between two *Chapters* than it is to drag and drop a Vellum file after a *Part* or *Volume*. Because instead of adding the Vellum file after the *Volume* or *Part*, it is added *to* the *Volume* or *Part*.

For example, look at the *Navigator* below...

I usually flesh out the front matter and back matter during this step as well.

Step 5 - Dragging and Dropping

Using Finder, drag each of your Vellum files created during the prep work into Vellum's *NAVIGATOR*. One by one, drop each of the files between two *Chapters*...

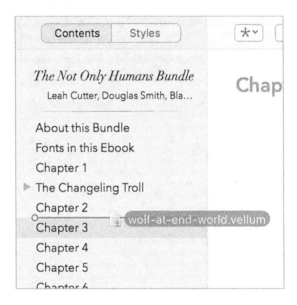

When you drop the file, Vellum will ask whether you want to use the book cover for the new *Volume*...

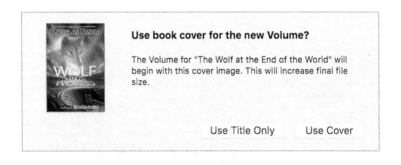

If you're worried about the final size of the bundle, click the **USE TITLE ONLY** button. This will create a *Title Page* for the *Volume* in the book. Otherwise the cover image will appear at the beginning of the *Volume*.

Including images in your book increases the size of your ebook.

NOTE

In Vellum 2.0.6, there is no way to change your decision to use the cover for the Volume. If you decide to use covers and then change your mind, or vice versa, you'll need to delete the Volume from your box set and re-drag and drop the Vellum file again, answering the question differently the second time.

One of the size considerations is with ebook pricing at Amazon. The size of the MOBI determines the minimum list price. For the USD currency, at the 35% royalty rate, the size breakdowns are:

- If the MOBI is less than 3 megabytes, the minimum list price is $0.99.
- If the MOBI is between 3 and 10 megabytes, the minimum list price is $1.99.
- If the MOBI is greater than 10 megabytes, the minimum list price is $2.99.

Note that the size requirement is not based on the size of the MOBI Vellum generates. Vellum includes multiple versions of your book in the MOBI you upload to KDP. After Amazon processes your uploaded MOBI, you can see the file size on the pricing screen.

After dropping the Vellum file into the box set and answering the cover question, click on the gear icon at the top left of the *Text Editor* and choose Add Author...

This will allow you type in the author's name under the *Volume's* heading. And then the author's name will appear in the *Table of Contents* next to their *Volume*.

Step 6 - Cleanup

Once all the volumes have been added to your box set, there just a few things left to do before you're finished.

First, delete all the placeholder *Chapters* from the *Navigator*. They're no longer needed.

Next, visually inspect the box set's *Title Page* in the *Navigator* and make sure you typed in all the author names correctly. Then inspect the *Table of Contents* and make sure each author's name appears and is correct, and nothing looks out of place.

———

Watch out for *Blurbs* and *Also By Elements*.
They can be pesky.

One mistake that can sneak into your box set is the wrong author name on a *Blurb* or *Also By*. This occurs when a Volume you add to your box set has a default heading for a *Blurb* or *Also By*. When those *Elements* have a default heading, Vellum will construct the heading from the author name set in the *Book Info*. (See **Chapter 5 – The Title Info**.) Since the author name is likely different in the box set's *Book Info* than it was from the imported Vellum file, the headings can have the wrong author name.

If you discover this when inspecting the *Table of Contents*, you'll need to go into the *Volume* and manually add the heading to the *Blurb* or *Also By*.

—————

Finally, flesh out any front matter or back matter that needs it.

Step 7 - Ebook Generation

Now you're ready to generate your ebooks as explained in **Chapter 16 – Generating Ebooks**.

NINETEEN

What Vellum Cannot Do

This chapter explains a few things Vellum cannot do.

Tables

The current version of Vellum (2.0.6) cannot produce tables in your books. Although this isn't generally a big deal with fiction, tables are used frequently in non-fiction books.

If you must have a table, convert the table to an image and add it to your book as an *Inline Image*.

Footnotes

Nope. Can't do them in Vellum and there's no easy workaround.

Internal Links

Often ebooks will have Internal Links that will link to another part of the ebook. The reader can click on the link and immediately jump to that area of the ebook.

Vellum doesn't support Internal Links.

Fine-Grained Tuning

Being a programmer, I often want to get under the hood and tweak things just so. Maybe have some text highlighted. Maybe a title that displays three times taller than the surrounding text.

Vellum doesn't allow these types of edits.

But in the long run, given everything that Vellum can do—and how well it does them—I'm willing to live with the inconvenience of not being able to tweak these small things.

TWENTY

Tips and Tricks

This chapter contains a number of tips and tricks that I've found useful with Vellum.

The Non-Breaking Space Trick

S ometimes it's nice to add a little vertical space in your books. Maybe you want a little more white space between two paragraphs. Or maybe you want to push the text at the bottom of a printed page down just a bit so an important section starts at the top of the next page.

The problem is no matter how many times you hit enter to add blank paragraphs in the *Text Editor*, only a single empty paragraph will appear in the *Preview*. You could have an entire page full of blank paragraphs in the *Text Editor* but the generated ebook only has a single blank line.

The answer is the **NON-BREAKING SPACE.**

A non-breaking space is a special whitespace character that acts a little differently than a normal space. And a paragraph in the *TEXT EDITOR* that contains a non-break space will become a paragraph in both the *PREVIEW* and your generated ebook. A paragraph containing an invisible character.

Voila! A little vertical space.

In other words, you now can have blank paragraphs in your ebook or print book.

So how can you type a non-breaking space?

There's an easy way and a hard way. The easy way is to hold the OPTION key down while hitting the SPACEBAR.

If that works for you, then great! But if you have the OPTION+SPACEBAR mapped to something else on your computer, you're going to have to use the hard way.

The hard way is to copy and paste a non-breaking space. Here are the instructions:

1. Open up the Wikipedia page for Non-breaking space in your web browser.
2. Look for the text in the first paragraph: a **non-breaking space** (" ").
3. On your web browser, highlight that space between the quotations with your mouse.
4. Press CMD+C to copy that space.
5. In Vellum's *TEXT EDITOR*, go to a blank paragraph and hit CMD+V to paste the space.

That's it. You've copied a non-breaking space into Vellum.

Whichever method you use, you now can create as many paragraphs as you want, each with nothing but a single non-breaking space. And you'll have additional vertical space in your book.

Be careful though! If you decide to remove them, they can be hard to find. (They're invisible.)

Don't Have "Untitled" or Empty Elements in Your Ebooks

Before generating ebooks, make sure there are no *Elements* with the heading "Untitled," and make sure every *Element* has some text content. *Parts* and *Volumes* do not need text content because they're not actually empty. They contain other *Elements*.

Some ebook stores will not publish your book if either of these conditions exist. I won't say which ebook store is a stickler on these two issues, but I will give you a hint: their name rhymes with "Pie-Books."

Repurpose Blurbs for Pre-Title Pages

This was mentioned back in **Chapter 8 – The Title Page**, but it bears repeating.

If you want a page to appear in your book before the *Title Page*, add a *Blurb* as the first *Element* of your book and change its heading to whatever you need. *Blurbs* don't have to actually contain sales blurbs.

How to Check if Your Book Contains Certain Features

If you want to see if you're using a certain feature, such as *Ornamental Breaks*, check your *Book Style* screen. Remember, the styles in the *Navigator* that are bold-faced indicate they are being used.

How to Import an EPUB or MOBI into Vellum

- Step 1 – Install Calibre from https://calibre-ebook.com/
- Step 2 – Add the EPUB or MOBI to your Calibre library.
- Step 3 – In Calibre, CONVERT the book and for the OUTPUT FORMAT choose RTF.
- Step 4 – Use the technique described in **Chapter 15 – Exporting to RTF** to convert the RTF to a DOCX.
- Step 5 – Import the DOCX into Vellum.
- Step 6 – Go through the book in Vellum and clean up what's needed.

Why convert to a RTF when Calibre can convert to a DOCX?

I've had better luck this way. More Text Features seem to be picked up. Your mileage may vary. Try it both ways and see which works best for you.

Tweak Font Family, Font Size, and Line Spacing for Your Print Books

Don't forget about that BODY style screen. Try different settings and generate your print file. You can print a few pages of the PDF on your printer to see what combinations are most readable.

A little time spent tweaking these setting locally can save you days of ordering proofs, changing your mind, and having to re-order proofs.

But your final judgment should always be made when reviewing a physical book in your hands.

Using Alignment Blocks at the Top of Chapters to Force Where the Drop Cap Appears

Sometimes you'll have a time, person, or location sub-heading at the top of your chapter and you don't want the drop cap to appear on it.

You could add them as a *Chapter* subtitle or a Subhead, but let's assume you don't like those two options for your book.

Just wrap your sub-heading in an *Alignment Block*. You can justify the Alignment Block to the left if you don't want it centered.

Vellum will skip past any text at the top of a *Chapter* that has an *Alignment Block* and apply drop caps to the first paragraph of normal text. (But only if your FIRST PARAGRAPH style uses drop caps.)

Save Common Elements in a Separate Vellum File

When you're creating multiple ebooks, it can save you a load of time if you keep common *Elements* to a separate Vellum file. Things like *About the Author*, *Also By*, or any other *Element* you commonly add to your books.

When you're creating a new book, open up two Vellum files at once: the new one and the one containing your common *Elements*. Then drag and drop each *Element* you want to the new book.

Or, you can simply open your common file in Vellum and choose FILE > DUPLICATE from Vellum's menu. Then rename the file and then just drag and drop your DOCX into the *NAVI-GATOR* to import your chapters. (Hat tip to Dayle Dermatis for this tip.)

This means you can create an *Also By* once, spending the time going through each of your books and entering *Store Links*. And then each time you have a new book, just copy that *Also By* including all embedded *Store Links*.

TWENTY-ONE

Using MacinCloud

This chapter discusses creating ebooks using Vellum with MacinCloud.

What is MacinCloud?

I t's an online service where you rent a Mac computer in the cloud.

They have several plans; the cheapest is the Pay-As-You-Go plan, which costs $1 per hour.

How It Works

You run special software on your local Windows, Linux, or Mac computer that allows you to control your "instance" of a MacinCloud computer.

If you're a Windows user, then you already have this special software installed. It's called MICROSOFT REMOTE DESKTOP. If you have a Mac, you can install MICROSOFT REMOTE DESKTOP from the App store. For Linux, you'll need to install RDESKTOP.

How Do You Share Files?

The easiest way to share files between your local computer and your MacinCloud computer is to use a service such as Dropbox, Microsoft OneDrive, or Apple iCloud.

TIP

Only share a single folder between your local computer and MacinCloud computer. You don't want to waste time synchronizing files that aren't needed on your MacinCloud computer.

How to Get Started

Point your browser to https://www.macincloud.com and go through the signup process...

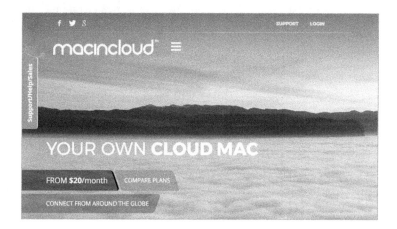

After you select your plan and create an account (they require your credit card info), you'll be emailed a welcome email.

This email contains your username, password, instructions, and a link to a zip file containing several connection files. These connection files make it easy to connect to your Macin-Cloud service. Just double-click on one of the connection files and you'll be connected to your MacinCloud computer, ready for you to enter the username and password to log on.

What to do First

The first thing I suggest doing is setting up your file sharing service. All the standard ones are pre-installed on your Macin-Cloud computer. You'll have to pick one, run the file sharing app on your MacinCloud computer, and log on to the file sharing service.

It's also a good idea to have your preferred file sharing app start automatically when you log on to your MacinCloud computer.

I also suggest you drag Vellum from the MacinCloud Launchpad to the Dock to make it easy to access. Yes, Vellum is pre-installed on your MacinCloud computer.

Basic Workflow using MacinCloud

Here's a basic workflow for using Vellum with MacinCloud.

1. Prepare your DOCX on your local computer. When you're ready to create your books, copy your DOCX to the folder you're sharing with MacinCloud
2. Log on to your MacinCloud computer.

3. Wait for the DOCX to appear in the shared folder on your MacinCloud computer.
4. Drag the DOCX to the Vellum icon on the dock to import the DOCX.
5. Perform any necessary edits in Vellum.
6. Generate your ebooks and/or print book.
7. Wait for the shared files from your MacinCloud computer to synchronize locally.
8. Log off your MacinCloud computer. NEVER FORGET TO DO THIS. You are charged while your MacinCloud computer is on, even if you aren't connected to it.

Voila!

Also by Chuck Heintzelman

Short Stories

Freshly Ghost

The Jaws of the Manō

The Train Bandits

Tailfeathers Up, Beak Down

Pact of the Banshee

Wizard Lottery

City Shadows

And Through the Haze You See Your God

Mad Goldilocks

Three Strikes

The Babysitter

The Djin's Box

It Don't Taste Like Slug

The Luckiest Man in the Universes

Memory Fades

Trunk of Caramel

Three Wishes and a Bath

Cleopatra's Medallion

The Death Gerbil

The Messiah Machine

Collections

Stuttering in the Dark

Expelled Figments

Non Fiction

Getting Stuff Done with Laravel 4

Laravel 5.1 Beauty

The Author's Guide to Ebook Bundling

The Author's Guide to Vellum

About the Author

 His short stories are stunning.

USA Today Bestselling author Dean Wesley Smith

Chuck has over three decades of experience developing software. He's created systems for businesses ranging from Fortune 500 companies to Mom and Pop stores. His latest project is BundleRabbit.com, a service that allows authors to promote their books in DIY bundles and readers to get more ebooks for less money.

When he's not writing code, Chuck writes quirky short stories, usually with some sort of fantastical element. He's as surprised by this as anyone. Even after dozens of stories published he still stays up too late at night, feverishly working on the next tale.

He lives in the Pacific Northwest with his beautiful wife and their daughters.

For more information:

StoryChuck.com
chuck@storychuck.com

About BundleRabbit

BundleRabbit is the premier DIY ebook bundling service. We help readers save money on ebooks by providing authors with the tools to bundle their books together and offer them at a discount.

BundleRabbit also provides an amazing service for multi-author projects:

Collaborative Publishing

With collaborative publishing co-authors can publish their books (ebook and print) without the headache of tracking and splitting royalties.

Visit BundleRabbit.com to discover more.

THE WITCHES'S BREW BUNDLE

Magic sparks and cauldrons bubble;

Potions bring love, and curses bring trouble.

What if magic could help track down a murderer?

Can a young, untrained witch save her people from a dark wizard –
and at what cost to herself?

Does a young woman's dreams really predict the future? If so, is there
any way to change what she foresees?

And what might an independent young witch look for when house
hunting?

Witches. Warlocks. Wizards. Familiars…

Enter twenty different worlds of magic and enchantment.

THE OUT OF THIS WORLD BUNDLE

Explore the future and the universe with this exciting bundle of science fiction & fantasy short stories, novellas, and novels. Discover how people will survive, and thrive, as they encounter challenges in outer space or deal with struggles here on Earth.

Mystery and adventure, drama and fear, technology and magic, all have their place in these exciting speculative stories.

Blast away with these 16 fantastical tales to parts unknown and out of this world!

THE FANTASY IN THE CITY BUNDLE

What if magic were right in front of you every day, but hidden from your sight?

For all you know, it is.

Maybe the reason you love the tasty creations from the nearby chocolate shop is that one of the ingredients is magic.

Perhaps some of the dreadlocks of the beautiful young girl you saw at the grocery store are snakes, not hair.

The woman you just passed on the street appeared to be on her cell phone, but she might really be speaking with a ghost.

How do you know for sure?

Witches. Ghosts. Faeries. Monsters. Magic...

Enter twenty different worlds, each with a different flavor of magic.

This bundle contains 20 urban fantasy stories about hidden magic in everyday life.

DISCOVER THESE AND MANY MORE BUNDLES AT
BUNDLERABBIT.COM